THE BIBLE
As a Key to Life

ERNEST "TUT" GROOVER

© 2020 Divine Works Publishing LLC.
THE BIBLE AS A KEY TO LIFE

ALL RIGHTS RESERVED. No part of this publication may be reproduced, stored in a retrieval system, or transmitted in any form or by any means, electronic, mechanical, photocopying, recording or otherwise without the prior permission of the publisher or in accordance with the provisions of the Copyright, Designs, and Patents Act 1988 or under the terms of any license permitting limited copying issued by the Copyright Licensing Agency.

The views expressed in this work are solely those of the author and do not necessarily reflect the views of the publisher, the publisher hereby disclaims any responsibility for them.

Printed in the United States of America
First Edition: 2020

Scripture taken from the King James Version®., (unless otherwise noted), Copyright © 1982 by Thomas Nelson. Used by permission. All rights reserved.

ISBN: 978-1-949105-21-6 (Paperback)
ISBN: 978-1-949105-22-3 (eBook)

Published by:
Divine Works Publishing, LLC
Royal Palm Beach, Florida USA

www.DivineWorksPublishing.com
561-990-BOOK (2665)

ACKNOWLEDGMENT AND DEDICATION

This book is dedicated to my mother, Wardell Groover; My grandparents, Tom Groover, Alice Groover, Charlie Lane and Ruby Lane. My mother was a great blessing to my earthly life. I learned from my mother what it means to love and respect others. Observing her personally inspired my life in countless ways, not to mention, she was an excellent cook.

My grandparents were also excellent role models. Tom Groover was a quiet and godly man, he lived by the word of God. Alice Groover, although small in stature, had a lot of spunk. She was always willing to lend a helping hand.

Charlie Lane was a great Baptist minister. He was filled with wisdom and biblical insight, he taught me the value of how to save a dollar. Ruby Lane was an excellent homemaker with a beautiful voice when she sang.

A special thank you to Mrs. Cora Sutton, my dear friend and sister in Christ. I appreciate her assistance with writing this book.

A thank you to my cousin and brother in Christ, Fred Lovelle, for all of his assistance with this book.

A special thank you to my sister, Lynda Groover, for all of her assistance in completing this book.

I would like to dedicate chapter 6 "What is the meaning of life?" To my dear friend, Don Masterson, who has a special sense of humor about life.

I give God all the glory, all the praise, and all the honor for inspiring me to write this book.

May this book glorify God the Father, God the Son and God the Holy Spirit.

TABLE OF CONTENTS

Introduction | ix

Chapter 1 How it All Began | *1*

Chapter 2 After the New birth, Then What? | *5*

Chapter 3 The Battle Rages | *17*

Chapter 4 Humankind | *21*

Chapter 5 The Bible A Guide | *25*

Chapter 6 What's the Meaning of Life? | *27*

Chapter 7 Free Will or Freedom of Choice | *31*

Chapter 8 Obedience, The Key to God's Blessing | *41*

Chapter 9 Why Was the Bible Given to Mankind? | *47*

Chapter 10 The Three Major Decisions in Life | *53*

Chapter 11 Jesus, the Man Who Mastered Life | *59*

About the Author | 65

INTRODUCTION

I believe, without a shadow of doubt that the Bible is the key to life. I believe it is the key that unlocks success in every area of life. I believe the Bible was given to mankind for a greater purpose than we've fully come to comprehend. I believe one can come to know the Creator intimately and personally as we can seek His face for guidance. I believe as a person practices the word of God and becomes a doer of the word, he will recognize that the Bible holds the key to a blessed life. Most of all, I believe the Bible is the inspired Word of the True and Living God. I hope this book will be a blessing to all who read it.

CHAPTER ONE

HOW IT ALL BEGAN

The Bible is composed of sixty-six books, beginning with Genesis and ending with Revelation. The Book of Genesis gives a clear picture of how God created the earth. In order for the Bible to be the guide or key to life, one must be born again as outlined in the book of Romans:

Romans 10:9 *That if thou shalt confess with thy mouth the Lord Jesus, and shalt believe in thine heart that God hath raised him from the dead, thou shalt be saved.*

Romans 10:10 *For with the heart man believeth unto righteousness; and with the mouth confession is made unto salvation.*

The new birth is the key to a great adventure with Christ. There are four basic or fundamental things to which a person must adhere to in order to become a child of God: *#1 Hear, #2 Believe, #3 Repent and #4 Confess.*

#1. Hear: A person must hear the divine word of God. One cannot become a child of God without hearing the word of God. By Hearing God's word, faith will come. God has something with-

in His word that will produce faith. Faith, by hearing and hearing by the word of God.

> **Roman 10:14** *How then shall they call on him in whom they have not believed? And how shall they believe in him of whom they have not heard? And how shall they hear without a preacher?*

#2. Believe: once a person hears the word of God, he must believe. God does not require one to understand everything, explain everything, or know everything. He does, however, require one to believe and act upon that which he believes, in faith, that which is intangible, which is invisible, and that which one cannot calculate mentally or intellectually—one must believe! Some people might argue it is hard to believe the Bible, but wait a minute, it is not hard to believe the Bible. Let me prove it to you. Let me ask you this simple question. Do you believe George Washington was the first president of the United States of America? I believe he was and I believe you will agree with me. You and I were not born at that point in human history, neither were your parents or grandparents or great-grandparents. Therefore, we must believe that George Washington was the first president of the United States of America. That which you do not know, you must believe. Remember, God does not require you to know everything, understand everything, or explain everything, but he does require you to believe an act upon what you believe, in faith.

 # 3. Repent: Repentance is necessary in order for a person to become a child of God. To repent means to turn away from; in other words, if one is going south on I-95, he turns around and goes the opposite way—north on I-95 instead; That's what repentance means. In other words, the person has decided not to practice sin as a way of life, he is willing to go the opposite way. No one is perfect in the sense of being flawless. However, his mind is made up to strive or attempt to do the right things in life. He has decided to follow the ways of God to the very best of his ability.

Luke 13:3 *I tell you nay, but except ye repent, ye shall all likewise perish.*

Acts 8:22 *Repent therefore of this thy wickedness, and pray God, if perhaps the thought of thine heart may be forgiven thee.*

#4 Confess: One must confess and acknowledge Jesus Christ as his own personal Lord and Savior. He must say this confession from his heart (or Spirit); in other words, believe Jesus Christ died for his sins, and make this confession with everything from within oneself. From one's innermost being, confession is saying that he desires Jesus Christ to be Lord and Savior of his life. Confession is a biblical principle pronounced throughout the word of God—the book which equips man with the greatest of spiritual wisdom, knowledge, and insight.

Proverbs 28:13 *He that covereth his sins shall not prosper, but whoso confesseth and forsaketh them shall have mercy.*

CHAPTER TWO

AFTER THE NEW BIRTH, THEN WHAT ?

Once a person is born again, he needs to be taught how to live according to biblical standards. That is the reason God placed the five-fold ministry gifts within the church or body of Christ. The five-fold ministry gifts are apostles, prophets, evangelists, pastors, and teachers.

> **Ephesians 4:11** *And he gave some, apostles; and some, prophets; and some, evangelists; and some, pastors and teachers;*

Apostles, prophets, evangelists, pastors, and teachers were placed in the church to edify and build up the body of Christ until we all come into the unity of the faith.

> **Ephesians 4:12** *For the perfecting of the Saints, for the work of the ministry, for the edifying of the body of Christ,*
> **13** *Till we all come into the unity of the faith, and of the knowledge of the Son of God, unto a perfect man, unto the measure of the stature of the fullness of Christ;*
> **14** *That we henceforth be no more children, tossed*

to and fro, and carried about with every wind of doctrine, by the sleight of men, and cunning craftiness, whereby they lie in wait to deceive;
15 *But speaking the truth in love, may grow up into him in all things, which is the head, even Christ;*
16 *From whom the whole body fitly joined together and compacted by that which every joint supplieth, according to the effectual working in the measure of every part, maketh increase of the body unto the edifying of itself in love.*

I have a very important point I would like to make here, please listen very closely. When a person is born again, the only thing that is affected is his spirit. His soul and body have not been affected by the new birth. It is true that Christ has fully paid the price for the total man: spirit, soul, and body. Yet, while man functions here in the earth realm, his body and soul have not been affected by the new birth. With this new birth experience there is a God-ward side and there is a man-ward side. Man plays a part or role in this new adventure, it is not just automatic. God has designed this new relationship to work that way. Nothing in life is merely automatic. Nothing I mean nothing! I believe with all my heart if Christians are taught about the three-fold nature of man, it would help us in our relationship or walk with the Lord. This is a very critical area concerning the new birth. **Here is a breakdown of the human personality.**

Spirit	**Soul**	**Body**
Righteousness	*Mind*	*See*
Revelation	*Intellect*	*Touch*
Communication	*Will*	*Taste*
Intuition	*Desires*	*Smell*
Conscience	*Moods*	*Hear*
	Feelings	
	Thoughts	
	Ideas	
	Emotions	

Now, think about this for a moment! If every part of one's three-fold nature were saved at the new birth, he would not sin once he became a Christian. You and I both know that is not true. We've all sinned since becoming Christians. First, John 1:9 was written to the Christian for this purpose:

1John 1:9 *If we confess our sins, God is faithful to forgive our sins and cleanse us from all unrighteousness.*

My friends, the only thing that is affected at the new birth is your spirit. Your soul and body have not yet been affected. I believe, it is God's desire and plan that our recreated spirit dominate and control our soul and body. However, we may have not been taught this spiritual truth. I believe that is why so many Christians fall into all kinds of sin. We have not been taught that our spirit should dominate and control our soul and body. If we are correctly taught this spiritual truth, it will help keep us out of trouble. God communicates with man through man's spirit not his soul or body.

Romans 8:16 *The Spirit itself beareth witness with our spirit, that we are children of God.*

1 Corinthians 6:17 *But he that is joined unto the Lord is one spirit.*

2 Corinthians 3:6 *Who also hath made us able ministers of the New Testament, not the letter, but of the spirit; for the letter killeth, but the Spirit giveth life.*

Mark 14:38 *Watch ye and pray, lest ye enter into temptation. The spirit truly is ready, but the flesh is weak.*

Man receives divine revelation knowledge from God through man's recreated human spirit. There is a knowledge higher than academic knowledge, which is called revelation knowledge. Revelation knowledge comes from God.

> **Romans 16:25** *Now to him that is of power to establish you according to my Gospel and the preaching of Jesus Christ according to the <u>revelation</u> of the mystery which was kept secret since the world began.*

> **2 Corinthians 12:1** *It is not expedient for me, doubtless to glory, I will come to vision and <u>revelation</u> of the Lord.*

Righteousness in its simplest definition, means right standing with God. When a person is born again God sees that person as being righteous. No, the person does not have any righteousness of his own, but God sees him that way once he becomes A Christian. Righteous is a trait one has from God at the time of the new birth.

> **Psalms 1:6** *For the lord knoweth the way of the righteous; but the way of the ungodly shall perish.*

> **Psalms 37:16** *A little that a righteous man hath is better than the riches of many wicked.*

> **1 Peter 3:12** *For the eyes of the Lord are over the righteous and his ears are open until their prayers, but the face of the Lord is against them they do evil.*

> **1 John 2:1** *My little children, these things write I unto you that you sin not, and if any man sin, we have an advocate with the Father Jesus Christ the righteous.*

Intuition is knowing something for a fact, not guessing or not being sure, intuition is knowing the will of God about a particular thing.

Conscience is the ability to know right from wrong. One's conscience will let him know when he is about to do something wrong. One's conscience is a safe guide as long as one is anchored in the word of God. (Read Acts and Romans).

> **Acts 24:16** *And in this do I exercise myself, to have always a conscience void of a fence toward God, and toward men.*

> **Romans 2:15** *Who show the work of the law written in their hearts, their conscience also bearing witness, and their thoughts the meanwhile accusing or else excusing one another.*

Let's talk about the soul of man. It is sad, but most Christians live in the soul part of the human personality. Remember, the soul is not saved yet while we function here in the earth realm. If we allow the soul to dominate, most of the time our soul will lead us away from the things and ways of God. The Bible tells us to do something about our soul.

> **1 Peter 2:11** *Dearly beloved, I beseech you as strangers and Pilgrims abstain from fleshly lusts, which war against the soul.*

> **3 John 1:1** *The elder until the well-beloved Gaius whom I love in the truth.*
> **1:2** *Beloved I wish above all things that thou mayest prosper and be in health even as thy soul prospereth.*

Notice how the word soul is used in 3 John 1:2. In order for the soul to prosper, the spirit man must be in control and dominate the soul part of man. God wants us to prosper in our soul nature. When we prosper in our soul nature we become winners in this life while we live upon planet earth.

The Bible instructs us to renew our mind. Remember, the mind is part of our soul nature.

> **Romans 12:2** *And be not conformed to this world, but be transformed by the renewing of your mind that you, may prove what is the good and acceptable and perfect will of God.*

> **Romans 8:6** *For to be carnally minded is death, but to be spiritually minded is life and peace.*

Because the Carnal mind is enmity against God, for it is not subject to the law of God. Neither indeed can be. So then they that are in the flesh cannot please God.

If a born-again Christian does not renew his mind with the word of God, he or she would basically end up living a defeated life as a Christian. He must program his mind with new information found in God's word. He must take the old information gained when he was in the world out of his mind. He must feed his born-again man new information, based on God's Holy Word. Remember, every thought that comes to one's mind will not be from God. This is one area Satan will attack very, very, very, often; thus, his thought life is an important area to guard against the enemy (which is Satan).

Feelings, emotions, and desires are the areas we must guard against. This area is a playground for Satan. He will attack us constantly in this area of our being. We must forever be on guard against the enemy.

Feelings, emotions, and desires.

> **Genesis 27:12** *and my father peradventure will <u>feel</u> me and I shall seem to him as a deceiver and I shall bring a curse upon me and not a blessing...*
> **21** *And Isaac said onto Jacob, "come near I pray thee that I may <u>feel</u> thee, my son, whether thou be my very son Esau or not."*
> **22** *And Jacob went near onto Isaac, his father, and he <u>felt</u> him and said, "The voice is Jacob's voice, but the hands are the hands of Esau."*

In this particular story we find a man who is deceived by his feelings. I would like to emphasize the importance of feelings, emotions, and desires. Isaac was deceived by his feelings. His son Jacob stole the blessings that were due, his brother, Esau. Isaac was not able to discern Jacob because he had false hair on his hands. I repeat, we must be on guard against feelings, emotions, and desires. This is a critical area if we want to walk in the things and in the ways of God. This is Satan's number one way to attack us as Christians. Be very careful in this area, it is a must.

I am not implying that we do not have feelings, emotions, or desires; we all have them. God made us with them; they are built into our three-fold nature. However, we must focus upon Godly desires, emotions and feelings.

> **1 Timothy 3:1** *This is a true saying if a man <u>desire</u> the office of a bishop he desireth a good work.*

> **Hebrew 11:16** *But now they <u>desire</u> a better country that is in heavenly, where for, God is not ashamed to be called their God for he has prepared for them a city.*

THE BIBLE AS A KEY TO LIFE

> **Luke 22:31** *And the lord said, "Simon, Simon behold Satan has desired to have you that he may sift you as wheat"*

Remember, your (our) Soul nature is not born again yet, while we live here on planet earth. Feelings, emotions, and desires are part of your (our) Soul nature.

Thinking—we must learn to think the way God thinks. Our thinking should be in line with God's Holy Word. The Bible tells us to think about <u>certain</u> things.

> **Phillipians 4:8** *Finally, brethren Whatsoever things are true, whatsoever things are honest, whatsoever things are pure, whatsoever things are lovely, whatsoever things are of good report; if there be any virtue and if there be any praise <u>think</u> on these things.*

We must endeavor to think God's thoughts and not the thoughts of the world system. Our thinking must be God centered.

> **Proverbs 23:74** *For as he <u>thinketh</u> in his heart, so is he.*

> **Matthew 9:4** *And Jesus knowing their thoughts said "wherefore <u>think</u> ye evil in your hearts."*

When we think on these things we can rest for sure that we are pleasing our Heavenly Father. Think Holy thoughts and you will be Holy. The opposite is think on unholy thoughts and you will be unholy.

Moods—we all have different moods at different times. Yet, this too is an area we must guard against. Satan will try to hinder in this area also. He will make every attempt to try to keep us from performing at our highest level.

The Will—The ability to say yes or no or maybe. Everybody's will is at a different level some people have stronger will power than others. The will is a very powerful component of the soul nature of man. The human will can make you or break you. Satan, also, will try to influence the will of man by trying to force or manipulate man to act against God's Holy Word.

> **Mark 3:35** *For whosoever shall do the <u>will</u> of God the same is my brother and my sister and mother.*
>
> **Acts 21:14** *And when he would not be persuaded, we ceased saying, The <u>will</u> of the Lord be done.*
>
> **1 Timothy 2:8** *I <u>will</u> therefore that men pray everywhere lifting up holy hands without wrath and doubting.*

Intellect—Intelligence is good, for God has no premium on ignorance.

> **1 Corinthians 14:38** *But if any man be <u>ignorant</u>, let him be ignorant.*
>
> **2 Corinthians 2:11** *Lest Satan should get an advantage of us for we are not <u>ignorant</u> of his devices.*
>
> **Acts 4:13** *Now when they saw the boldness of Peter and John, and perceived that they were unlearned and <u>ignorant</u> men, they marveled and took knowledge of them that they had been with Jesus.*

There is nothing wrong with being sharp or having knowledge about a particular subject matter. Knowledge is good within its proper context, however, remember, knowledge and intelligence can go only so far. We must ask God for wisdom and understanding in every area of life. Wisdom is the ability to take knowledge, information, facts, figures, and rightly apply them in any given situation or circumstance. Remember wisdom comes from God, not man.

> **James 1:5** *if any of you lack <u>wisdom</u>, let him ask of God that give it to all men liberally an upbraideth not and it shall be given him.*

> **Proverbs 4:7** <u>*Wisdom*</u> *is the principal thing therefore get wisdom and with all thy getting get understanding.*

> **1 Corinthians 1:30** *But of him are you in Christ Jesus who of God is made onto us <u>wisdom</u> and righteousness and sanctification and redemption.*

Remember, if you have wisdom, you have understanding; they go together like water is wet.

In summary on the soul nature of man. The soul of man will lead man away from the things and ways of God, unless the soul is directed by the spirit of man (that man's spirit is born-again) and again, we must know this great spiritual truth. In the book of Hosea, God said his people were destroyed for a lack of knowledge. The spirit of man and the soul of man are fighting against each other, which one will you let control your personality the choice is yours!

The body—we live in what we call a three dimensional physical world, that is composed of space energy and time. We contact our world with the five basic senses. With our bodies we contact our environment around us. Our physical bodies were made for this world, not Heaven. Man needs a physical body to function in this earth. The physical body of man is decaying day by day.

2 Corinthians 4:16 *For which cause we faint not, but the lower outward man parish yet the inward man is renewed day by day.*

A man's physical body house is his spirit and soul.

1 Corinthians 6:19 *What? Know ye not that your body is the temple of the Holy Spirit which is in you, which ye have of God and ye are not your own?* **20** *For you are bought with a price; therefore, glorify God in your body, and in your spirit, which are God's.*

The Bible declares that we have this treasure in earthen vessel (our body).

2 Corinthians 4:7 *But, we have this treasure in earthen vessels, that the excellency of the power may be of God, and not of us.*

We must take care of our bodies; we must eat properly; we must exercise; and we must get proper rest. Our physical bodies are very important to God; thus, we must do everything we can to take care of them.

In summary of the threefold nature of man: Man is a Trinity; Man has three parts: spirit, soul, and body. It is God's desire that man spirit dominate and control his soul and body. When we let our spirit dominate and control us, our lifestyles will be pleasing to the Lord.

CHAPTER THREE

THE BATTLE RAGES

Now, you are saved; you are born again; you are a new creation in Christ Jesus; you are heaven bound; and your names are written in the Lamb's Book of Life.

Philippians 4:3 *And I intreat thee also, true yokefellow, help those women which labored with me in the gospel with Clement also, and with other my fellow-laborers, whose names are in the Book of Life.*

Luke 10:20 *Notwithstanding, in this rejoice not, that the spirits are subject unto you, but rather rejoice because your names are written in heaven.*

Mankind has an enemy in life, which is Satan. Whether you are saved or unsaved you have an enemy in life. Once you are saved, Satan will do everything he can to try to turn you away from the things and ways of God. You must, without a shadow of doubt know that you have an enemy in life.

Satan knows he cannot hurt God, Jesus, or the Holy Spirit, and he knows God loves mankind in the earth realm. Satan will do everything he can to destroy you and me. God sent Jesus to die for you and me. Jesus defeated Satan on his own territory. Satan is referred to as the god of this world.

> **2 Corinthians 4:4** *In whom the god of this world has blinded the minds of them which believe not lest the light of the glorious gospel of Christ who is the image of God shine unto them.*

> **John 14:30** *Hereafter, I will not talk much with you for the prince of this world cometh and hath nothing in me.*

You must know that Satan is the god of this world system. He makes every attempt to try and break fellowship between God and man. Satan tries to enslave man with sin. Satan was an arch-angel in heaven; however, he was kicked out, along with all the other rebellious angels.

> **John 16:33** *These things have I spoken unto you that in me you might have peace. In the world ye shall have tribulation but be of good cheer, I have overcome the world.*

> **Galatians 1:4** *Who gave himself for our sins that he might deliver us from this present evil world, according to the will of our God and Father.*

We, as Christians, have authority over Satan and demons spirits. We have authority to use the name of Jesus in the earth realm. There is power in using the name of Jesus. When we use that name properly, every demon must move. Power is invested in the name of Jesus. Satan is not anybody's friend who resides in the earth realm. Satan is a thief; He came to steal, kill, and destroy. For approximately six thousand years, this great battle has been raging in the earth realm. It will not cease until Jesus comes back to set up his kingdom in the earth. We must fight the good fight of faith and exercise and use the mighty name of Jesus against the forces of darkness. In this life we will have trials, tests, temptations, and disappointments, but victory is still ours, as we seek God's leading and guidance. Therefore, let the battle rage on, for we as believers in the Lord Jesus Christ, will surely obtain the victory.

> **Luke 20:35** *But they which shall be accounted worthy to obtain that world, and the resurrection from the dead, neither marry, nor are given in marriage:*

CHAPTER FOUR

HUMANKIND

Man is a creature of time; he must deal with time whether he likes it or not. The way he spends his time is very important. The Bible states

Ephesians 5:16 *Redeeming the time, because the days are evil.*

Colossians 4:5 *Walk in wisdom toward them that are without, redeeming the time.*

Redeem the time because the days are evil. In essence, that means we must spend our time wisely in all our affairs. As I mentioned earlier, we live in what is called a three dimensional physical world consisting of: space, energy, and time. Time is one of those components. Time began at the start of creation. Day follows night, sunrise, sunset; seconds become minutes, minutes become hours, hours become days, days become weeks, weeks become months, and months become years. The element of time keeps moving. Someone said, the further one goes out into space, time ceases to exist. Once we reach heaven, time will no longer exist the way we know time in the earth today. If we polled one hundred Americans and asked how each one spends his time, we may get one hundred different answers. Each person spends his time doing different things in the course of a day. The Bible states:

> **Psalms 90:10** *The days of our years are threescore years and ten and if by reason of strength they be four score years yet is their strength labour and sorrow for it is soon cut off and we fly away.*

The Lord has granted us roughly around 70 or 80 years of life here in the earth realm. That is a promise the Lord has given mankind, in a general sense, concerning time.

The Bible States:

> **Revelation 2:21** *And I gave her space to repent of her fornication and she repented not.*

The Lord gave Jezebel a space to repent, and she repented not; that space involved time. The Bible states Joshua prayed and that time stopped.

> **Joshua 10:12** *Then spoke Joshua to the Lord in the day when the Lord delivered up the Amorites before the children of Israel and he said in the sight of Israel "Sun stand still upon Gibeon, and thou Moon, in the Valley of Aijalon."*
> *13 And the sun stood still, and the moon stayed until the people had avenged themselves upon their enemies. Is not this written in the book of Joshua? So the sun stood still in the <u>midst of heaven</u> and haste not to go down about a <u>whole day</u>.*
> *14 And there was no day like that before it or after it, that the Lord hearkened onto the voice of man, for the Lord fought for Israel.*

At one time or another, we have all made this statement, "If I had more time, I would do more things." The element of time is important; we have made the statement, "he or she was in the right place at the right time." Time is one of the most important things we possess while we live here in the earth realm.

CHAPTER FIVE

THE BIBLE, A GUIDE

There is no doubt in my mind that the Bible is the key to living our best life. The Bible is a guide for mankind to grasp while he/she lives up on planet earth. The word of God states that the Lord will lead and guide us into all truth

Psalms 31:3 *For thou art my rock and my fortress, therefore, for thy name's sake <u>lead</u> me, and <u>guide</u> me.*

John 16:13 *Howbeit when he, the Spirit of truth, is come, He will <u>guide</u> you into all truth…*

Isaiah 48:17 *Thus saith the Lord the Redeemer, the Holy One of Israel; I am the Lord thy God, which teacheth thee to profit, which leadeth thee by the way that thou shouldest go.*

When we follow God as our guide, we can rest and be assured, that everything will be all right. When God leads and guides us, we can be assured of peace, happiness, and joy. God's word is a guide to keep mankind on course with his Creator and fellow man. God will lead and guide us in every area of life, if we are willing and obedient and seek the things and ways of God. The pages of the Bible are filled with guiding principles from the Lord. Once we become children of God, we can really have this divine guidance. We should all be more sensitive to the leading and guiding of the Holy Spirit. The Holy Spirit acts as our guide while we live here in the earth realm, He, the Holy Spirit is the third person of the Godhead. Let's rely upon the guidance of God's Holy Word.

CHAPTER SIX

WHAT'S THE MEANING OF LIFE?

I assume that most of us have asked ourselves this very question. *What's the meaning of life?* That, of course, is a very broad question. Again, if we took a poll of 100 people in the United States of America, we may get 100 different answers to that particular question.

However it is answered, one thing remains constant; Life should have some meaning for us all while we live here on planet earth. Life's deeper meaning and purposes can unfold beautifully once we learn how to walk with the Lord. The following Scriptures teach us :

Proverbs 18:21 *Death and life are in the power of the tongue...*

Psalms 91:16 *With long life will I satisfy him, and show him my salvation.*

Luke 12:15 *And he said onto them take heed and beware of covetousness for a man's life consisted not in the abundance of the things which he possesses.*

Jesus said he came that we may have life and have it more abundantly. A person can have an abundant life only in Jesus Christ. That's why the gospel message is so important to mankind. (The Great Commission) Go out into the world and preach the gospel to every creature.

>**Matthew 4:23** *And Jesus went about all Galilee teaching and preaching the Gospel of the Kingdom...*

>**Mark 16:15** *And he said unto them, Go ye into all the world, and preach the gospel to every creature.*

>**Colossians 1:23** *If you continue in the faith grounded and settled and be not moved away from the hope of the gospel which ye have heard, which was preached to every creature which is under heaven whereof I Paul am made a minister;*

You will never know what life is all about until you come to Christ that's why man must be born again. Man must be born of God's Spirit. Nicodemus, a great ruler asked that question "How can a man be born again?"

>**1 John 5:1** *Whosoever believeth that Jesus is the Christ is born of God: and every one that loveth him that begat loveth him also that is begotten of him.*

>**1 Peter 1:23** *Being born again, not of corruptible seed, but incorruptible, by the word of God, which liveth and abideth forever.*

>**John 3:3** *Jesus answered and said unto him, verily, verily I say unto you except a man be born again, he cannot see the kingdom of God.*

> **4:** *Nicodemus said on to him, how can a man be born when he is old? Can he enter the second time into his mothers womb, and be born?*
>
> **5:** *Jesus answered, Verily, verily, I say unto thee, except a man be born of water and the spirit, he cannot enter into the kingdom of God.*

The new birth is a supernatural experience. It is the greatest occurrence that could happen to an individual while he or she lives upon planet earth. As I stated earlier, the new birth is the beginning of this adventure with Christ. When one is born again, his human spirit is connected to God's Holy Spirit; God's Spirit comes to take up residence within him. A person will never be totally fulfilled until he or she comes to Christ. I believe the gospel message is the singular most important thing up on planet earth. This message is all about life in Jesus Christ, the God-kind of life which can only be found in Jesus Christ. A completely fulfilled life comes only by way of knowing Jesus as one's personal Lord and Savior. I believe Christ is the answer for the entire world. Until mankind comes to that reality, he will never know what the meaning of life is all about. For life can have meaning and purpose only in Christ Jesus. When a person becomes Christ-minded, he is on his way to living victoriously (the only way to live). Life has meaning when we come to know Christ intimately and personally.

> **John 16:33** *These things have I spoken on to you, that in me you might have peace. In the world you shall have tribulation: but be of good cheer; I have overcome the world.*

> **Acts 14:22** *Confirming the souls of the disciples, and exhorting them to continue in the faith, and that we must through much tribulation enter into the kingdom of God.*

Jesus never said we would not experience trials in this life, but the true test is will we become overcomers in this life over all trials, problems, conflicts, or anything Satan throws at us?

Romans 8:37 *And in all these things we are more than conquerors through him that loved us.*

With life comes many challenges and temptations, but we have already attained the victory in Christ. We can only come to know this victory by walking closely with Jesus.

CHAPTER SEVEN

FREE WILL OR FREEDOM OF CHOICE?

God created man with the ability to make choices. I once heard someone say that all of life is made up of making choices.

Although we have this ability to choose, there is a *perfect* or decreed will of God as outlined in the Bible for mankind in a general sense. There's also a *permissive* will of God, choices that God allows man to make on his own. For example: the Bible states it is not the will of God that any man should perish

> **2 Peter 3:9** *The Lord is not slack concerning his promise, as some men count slackness; but is long-suffering to us-word, not willing that any one should perish, but that all should come to repentance.*

In other words, it is God's will that no person be eternally lost. However when you give a person freedom of choice, he or she may not agree with you on your terms. That's the risk factor involved when you deal with people on any terms in any given situation. Nevertheless, I believe God lets a person decide his or her own eternal destiny. That is an awesome responsibility, yet I believe it is biblically sound. I believe as you read from Genesis through Revelation, you will find mankind exercising his free will or freedom of choice. When God made Abraham the promise that he would become the father of many nations, I believe Abraham had a choice to take it or leave it.

> **Romans 4:20** *He staggered not at the promise of God through unbelief but was strong in faith, giving glory to God; and being fully persuaded that, what he had promised, he was able also to perform.*

The dispensation of promise started with Abraham. A dispensation in its simplest meaning is a particular time period in which God deals with mankind. God is presently dealing with us in the sixth dispensation which is of grace and truth. Throughout human history God has been dealing with mankind upon the earth. Another example, was when God instructed Noah to build the ark, I believe Noah also had a choice.

> **Genesis 6:13** *And God said unto Noah, the end of all flesh is come before me; for the earth is filled with violence through them; and, behold, I will destroy them with the earth.*
> **14** *Make me an ark of gopher wood; rooms shalt thou make in the ark, and shalt pitch it within and without with pitch.*
> **15** *And this is the fashion which thou shalt make it of: The length of the ark shall be three hundred cubits, the breadth of it 850 cubits, and a height of it thirty cubits.*
> **16** *A window shalt thou make to the ark, and in a cubit shalt thou finish it above; and the door of the ark shalt thou set in the side thereof; with lower, second, and third stories shalt thou make it.*
> **17** *And behold, I, even I, do bring a flood of waters upon the earth, to destroy all flesh, wherein is the breath of life, from under heaven; and every thing that is in the earth shall die.*

18 *But with thee will I establish my covenant; and thou shalt come into the ark, thou, and thy sons, and thy wife, and thy sons' wives with thee.*

God's heart should be at the forefront of our minds when we make tough life decisions and/or choices. It is very imperative for the Christian to seek God's face when confronting a crisis or any kind of problem. I believe Moses had a choice when God called him.

> **Exodus 3:3** *And Moses said, I will turn aside, and see this great site, why the bush is not burnt.*
> **4** *And when the Lord saw that he turned aside to see, God called onto him out of the mist of the bush, and said Moses, Moses. And he said, Here am I.*

> **Exodus 3:13** *And Moses said unto God, Behold when I come unto the children of Israel, and shall say unto them, The God of your fathers hath sent me on to you; and they shall say to me, What is his name? What shall I stay on to them?*
> **14** *And God said unto Moses, I Am That I Am: and he said Thus shalt thou say onto the children of Israel, I AM has sent me onto you.*

> Note: Read the entire of Exodus 3 carefully.

I believe Jonah had a choice when God called him, Jonah disobeyed God, and Jonah suffered the consequences.

> **Jonah 1:1** *Now the word of the Lord came onto Jonah the son of Amittai, saying,*
> **2** *Arise, go to Nineveh, that great city, and cry against it; for their wickedness is come up before me.*
> **3** *But Jonah, rose up to flee unto Tarshish from the pres-*

ence of the Lord, and went down to Joppa; and he found a ship going to Tarshish: so he paid for the fare thereof, and went down into it, to go with them unto Tarshish from the presence of the Lord.

I believe Sampson had a choice when he was called to deliver God's people. It was not wise for Sampson to get himself involved with Delilah, but he did. He made a choice.

Judges 13:24 *And the woman bore a son, and called his name Sampson: And the child grew, and the Lord blessed him.*
25 *And the Spirit of the Lord began to move him at times in the camp of Dan between Zorah and Eshtaol.*

Judges 14:1 *And Sampson went down to Timnath, and saw a woman in Timnath of the daughters of the Philistines.*
2 *And he came up and told his father and his mother, and said, I have seen a woman in Timnath of the daughters of the Philistines: now get her for me to wife*
3 *Then his father and his mother said onto him, is there never a woman among the daughters of thy brethren, or among all my people, that thou goest to take a wife of the uncircumcised Philistines? And Sampson said unto his father, get her for me; for she pleaseth me well.*
4 *But his father and mother knew not that it was of the Lord, that he sought an occasion against the Philistines: for at that time the Philistines had dominion over Israel.*

I believe David had a choice when he had an affair with Bathsheba.

2 Samuel 11:2 *and it came to pass in an evening tide, That David arose from his bed, and walked upon the roof of the kings house: and from the roof he saw a woman*

washing herself; and the woman was very beautiful to look upon.
3 And David sent and inquired after the woman. And one said, it's not this Bathsheba, the daughter of Eliam, the wife of Uriah the Hittite?
4 And David sent messengers, and took her; and she came in unto him, and he lay with her; for she was purified from her uncleanliness: and she returned unto her house.
5 And the woman conceived, and sent and told David, and said, I am with child.

When the twelve apostles were called, I believe they had a choice.

Acts 1:13 And when they were come in, they went into an upper room, where abode both Peter, and James, and John, and Andrew, Philip, and Thomas, Bartholomew, and Matthew, James the son of Alphaeus, and Simon Zelotes and Judas the brother of James.
14 These all continued with one accord in prayer and supplication, with the women, and Mary the mother of Jesus, and with his brethren.

Acts 1:26 And they gave forth their lots; and the lot fell upon Matthias; and he was numbered with the eleven apostles.

Acts 2:1 And when the day of Pentecost was fully come, they were all with one accord in one place.

Acts 2:4 And they were all filled with the Holy Ghost, and began to speak with other tongues, as the Spirit gave them utterance.

> **Acts 2:14** *But Peter, standing up with the eleven, lifted up his voice, and said to them, Ye men of Judea, and all ye that dwell at Jerusalem, be this known unto you, and hearken unto my words:*

Although Paul was a chosen vessel from God, I still believe he exercised his free will to follow God.

> **1 Corinthians 1:1** *Paul, called to be an apostle of Jesus Christ, through the will of God, and Sothenes our brother.*

I believe Peter had a choice when he denied Christ three times.

> **Mark 3:14** *And he ordained twelve, that they should be with him, and that he might send them forth to preach,*
> **15** *And to have power to heal sicknesses, and to cast out devils:*

> **Matthew 26:70** *But he denied before them all, saying, I know not what thou sayest.*

> **Matthew 26:72** *And again he denied with an oath, I do not know the man.*

I believe Judas had a choice when he sold Jesus for thirty pieces of silver.

> **Matthew 26:14** *Then one of the twelve, called Judas Iscariot, went unto the chief priests,*
> **15** *And said unto them, What will you give me, and I will deliver him unto you? And they covenanted with him for thirty pieces of silver.*
> **16** *And from that time he sought opportunity to betray him.*

Most of all, I believe our Lord and Savior, The Lord Jesus Christ had a choice when he left the glories of Heaven to come to Earth to redeem mankind upon planet Earth. The greatest choice ever made for mankind.

> **Matthew 26:39** *And he went a little further, and fell on his face, and he prayed, saying, O my Father, if it be possible, let this cup pass from me: nevertheless, not as I will, but as thou wilt.*

I believe the most important choice a person will make is when he or she except Jesus Christ as his personal Lord and Savior (the number-one choice of all).

Yes, I believe life is made up of the choices one makes. If you've never accepted Jesus Christ as your personal Lord and Savior, I invite you to say the simple prayer from your heart.

Dear Heavenly Father, I come to you in the most humble manner as I know how. Father, I confess Jesus Christ as my own personal Lord and Savior. Father, I ask you to forgive me of my sins. Father, I repent and I turn from sin as a way of life. I accept your son, Jesus Christ as my Savior and Lord. This is my prayer, Heavenly Father, from my heart. Heavenly Father, by faith I believe I am saved now. I thank you now, Father, for your Great Salvation. Amen.

> **Romans 10:9** *That if thou shall confess with thy mouth of the Lord Jesus, and shalt believe in thine heart that God hath raised him from the dead, thou shalt be saved.* **10:** *For with the heart man believeth unto righteousness; and with the mouth confession is made unto salvation.*

Yes, I'll say it again, I believe life is comprised of the choices we make. God bestows upon man responsibility for his own eternal destiny. Remember, earlier, I said there was a God-ward side and a man-ward side to this great experience called the new birth. The Bible states no man can come to God except the Spirit draws him. The Holy Spirit draws men and women. The Holy Spirit convicts a person that he should be saved. However, a person must exercise his will to accept or reject the gospel message. It does not happen automatically. The Bible states today is the day of salvation.

> **Luke 19:9** *And Jesus said unto him, This day is salvation come to this house, for so much as he also is a son of Abraham.*

> **Acts 16:17** *The same followed Paul and us, and cried, saying, These men are the servants of the most high God, which shew unto us the way of salvation.*

Salvation is a gift from God. There is nothing in the world one can do to earn this great gift. Nothing! Nothing! I mean nothing!

> **Ephesians 2:8** *For by grace are ye saved through faith; and that not of yourselves: it is the gift of God:* **9** *not of works, lest any man should boast.*

One cannot pay enough tithes and offerings; neither morals nor ethical behavior will save a person. Salvation is a gift from God to mankind. One may accept or reject it. It is that simple. God's grace alone is sufficient for one's salvation. Grace is God's unmerited favor or unearned favor for mankind. Man cannot purchase his salvation through good works; it will not work.

You may have heard this statement, "Good works will not produce salvation, but salvation will produce good works." That is a true statement!

FREE WILL OR FREEDOM OF CHOICE?

All mankind are creatures of God, but all mankind are not children of God. One can only become a child of God through the process of the new birth. That's the only way! One must accept Jesus Christ as his own personal Lord and Savior. Jesus Christ is the savior of the whole world, there is none other. Jesus is the one!! Jesus said, "No man can come to the father except through me."

John 14:6 *Jesus saith unto him, I am the way, the truth, and the life: no man cometh unto the father, but by me.*

The key to life is knowing Jesus Christ as one's own personal Lord and Savior. I pray and hope you will accept him today. The choice is yours!

CHAPTER EIGHT

OBEDIENCE, THE KEY TO GOD'S BLESSING

I believe obedience Is the key ingredient to God's blessing upon his people. The Bible declares that obedience is better than sacrifice.

1 Samuel 15:22 *And Samuel said, Hath the Lord as great delight in burnt offerings and sacrifices, as in obeying the voice of the Lord? Behold, to obey is better than sacrifice, and to hearken then the fat of rams.*

2 Corinthians 2:9 *For to this end also did I write, that I might know the proof of you, whether ye be obedient in all things.*

God requires obedience from his children, just as natural human parents should require obedience from their children. Obedience is a broad subject concerning God's Holy Word. Let us start off by talking about love.

Love

I believe love is the key ingredient if a person wants God's blessings upon his life while he lives up on planet Earth. It is very important for the child of God to walk in love. As the Bible declares, love covers a multitude of sins.

> **Romans 13:8** *Owe no man anything, but to love one another: for he that loveth another hath fulfilled the law.*

The God-kind of love lets one love his enemies and those who would mistreat him for no reason.

> **Luke 6:27** *But I say unto you which hear, Love your enemies, do good to them which hate you,*

Love is a powerful ingredient upon which the believer has to draw from. For God so loved the world, that He gave his only begotten Son that whosoever believes in Him should have everlasting life.

> **1 John 4:11** *Beloved, if God so loved us, we ought also to love one another....*

> **1 John 4:19** *We love Him, because He first loved us.*

The love of God has been shed abroad in our hearts. We must learn how to walk in love toward our fellowman. We should practice love on a daily basis.

We should be more lovable today than we were ten years ago. Love is something we should practice in any given situation. We can prevent a lot of heartaches and pains if we learn to walk in the God-kind of love. This love worketh no evil toward one's neighbor.

> **Matthew 22:39** .... *Thou shall love thy neighbor as thyself.*

We cannot fully understand the love God has for mankind when He sent His son to die for the sins of the whole world. That's the Greatest Love a person could ever experience. Mentally, we cannot comprehend that kind of love. When we love God and our fellowman, we can expect the blessing of God upon our lives. Love, is a key ingredient to God's blessings; then, when we practice love, we are being obedient to the Lord. Let us practice love in every area of our lives.

Joy

I believe joy is another key ingredient to God's blessing on a person's life. I believe a joyful person can be a blessed person. Joy is one of the fruits of the Spirit.

> **Galatians 5:22** *But the fruit of the Spirit is love, joy, peace, longsuffering, gentleness, goodness, faith,*
> **23** *Meekness, temperance: against such there is no law.*

A joyful person can be a blessing to other people with whom he associates. The Bible tells us to rejoice in the Lord always.

> **Phillipians 4:4** *Rejoice in the Lord always: and again I say, Rejoice.*

I believe joy is a characteristic of man's recreated human spirit. When a person is joyful, he or she can face trials and tests much easier than a non-joyful person can. To be joyful consistently means one can face life's problems with confidence in the True and Living God. I believe inner joy comes from our Lord. I believe He wants us to be joyful in all the affairs of our earthly lives. To be joyful is to have one's mind focused on the proper things in life.

The scripture tells us "Weeping may endure for a night, but joy comes in the morning."

Psalms 30:5 *Weeping may remain for a night, but rejoicing comes in the morning.*

Yes, I reiterate the fact that, I believe the Lord wants His people to be joyful in all affairs.

Faith

I believe faith is very important for the children of God if they are to receive His blessings. Faith is a powerful force which God has given to mankind. When we exercise faith, we can expect God to move on our circumstances and problems. God expects us to live by faith. We must exercise faith, if we are to live God's best.

When our faith is in God, we have a sure foundation. Our faith in God will cause God to move for us on our behalf. God is a faith God, and He expects us to live by faith.

Hebrews 4:24 *For unto us was the gospel preached, as well as unto them: but the word preached did not profit them, not being mixed with faith in them that heard it.*

1 Peter 1:7 *That the trial of your faith, being much more precious than of gold that perisheth, though it be tried with fire, might be found unto praise and honor and glory at the appearing of Jesus Christ:*

James 1:17 *Every good gift and every perfect gift is from above, and cometh down from the Father of lights, with whom is no variableness, neither shadow of turning.*

Romans 1:19 *Because that which may be known of God is manifest in them; for God hath shewed it unto them.*

20 *For the invisible things of him from the creation of the world are clearly seen, being understood by the things that are made, even his eternal power and Godhead; so that they are without excuse:*

Luke 7:50 *And he said to the woman, Thy faith has saved thee; go in peace.*

Patient or Patience

Patience involves time. I'll admit patience is sometimes difficult when we are waiting on the Lord to move in our lives. However, our heavenly father, wants us to be patient when we seek his help and guidance. We have microwave ovens, jumbo jets, computers etc. Since we are living in the information age, things can be done very quickly by merely pushing a few buttons. Yet, when it comes to the things and ways of God, sometimes there is a waiting period. We must wait on the Lord to move for us in any given situation. Patience, therefore becomes essential if we desire God's best. Patience can be explained as endurance and steadfastness. We should learn to be patient when we are believing in God for something. If we want to be obedient to our Heavenly Father, we must practice patience daily.

Luke 8:15 *But that on the good ground are they, which in an honest and good heart, having heard the word, keep it and bring forth fruit with patience.*

Romans 5:3 *And not only so, but we glory in tribulations also: knowing that tribulation worketh patience;*

2 Corinthians 6:4 *But in all things approving ourselves as the ministers of God, in much patience, in afflictions, in necessities, in distresses,*

James 1:3 *Knowing this, that the trying of your faith worketh patience.*

Revelations 14:12 *Here is the patience of the saints: here are they that keep the commandments of God, and the faith of Jesus.*

CHAPTER NINE

WHY WAS THE BIBLE GIVEN TO MANKIND?

I believe when God created man, His intent was for man to live a happy and blessed life upon planet earth. However, God made the first man Adam with a will (or free will). We know from scriptures that Adam had free will because he named all the other creatures God had made.

> **Genesis 2:19** *And out of the ground the Lord God formed every beast of the field, and every fowl of the air; and brought them unto Adam to see what he would call them, and whatsoever Adam called every living creature, that was the name there of.*
> **20** *And Adam gave names to all cattle, and to the fowl of the air, and to every beast of the field; but for Adam there was not found a help meet for him.*

We know from scripture that God gave Adam a help meet.

> **Genesis 2:21** *And the Lord God caused a deep sleep to fall upon Adam, and he slept: and he took one of his*

THE BIBLE AS A KEY TO LIFE

ribs, and closed up the flesh instead thereof;
22 *And the rib, which the Lord had taken from man, made he a woman, and he brought her unto the man.*
23 *And Adam said, This is now bone of my bones and flesh of my flesh: she shall be called Woman, because she was taken out of Man.*
24 *Therefore shall a man leave his father and his mother, and shall cleave unto his wife: and they shall be one flesh.*

We know the story of Adam and Eve and how they fell into sin. The Lord told him not to eat fruit from the tree of the knowledge of good and evil.

Genesis 3:1 *Now the serpent was more subtle than any beast of the field which the Lord God had made. And he said to the woman, Yea, hath God said ye shall not eat of every tree of the garden?*
2 *And the woman said unto the serpent, We may eat of the fruit of the trees of the garden:*
3 *But of the fruit of the tree which is in the midst of the garden, God hath said, Ye shall not eat of it, neither shall ye touch it, lest ye die.*
4 *And the serpent said unto the woman, Ye shall not surely die:*
5 *For God doth know that in the day you eat thereof, then your eyes shall be open, and you shall be as gods, knowing good and evil.*
6 *And when the woman saw that the tree was good for food, and that it was pleasant to the eyes, and a tree to be desired to make one wise, she took of the fruit thereof and did eat, and gave also unto her husband with her; and he did eat.*
7 *And the eyes of them both were open, and they knew that they were naked; and they sewed fig leaves togeth-*

er, and made themselves aprons.

Based upon these verses, I believe Adam had not eaten the fruit that Eve gave him, the Lord probably would have given him (Adam) another wife. We know that Adam joined Eve in disobeying God. Together, they sinned; they committed a terrible sin or high treason. They sold out on the great plan God had for mankind up on planet Earth. When this happened, the whole earth was affected, and all future humans who would live upon planet earth would be affected by this great sin. The length of their stay in the garden of Eden is referred to as the Dispensation of Innocence. Remember, earlier, I said dispensation, in its simplest definition, means a particular time period in which God deals with mankind up on planet Earth. God is all wise, and all knowing, and for approximately 6000 years, God has been leading man step-by-step.

After Adam and Eve sinned, God drove them out of the Garden of Eden. They became conscious of sin and wrong doing. This is referred to as the Dispensation of Conscience. Man has an enemy in life while he lives upon planet Earth. Satan is man's enemy. Satan hates God, and the only way he can hurt God is by deceiving man up on planet earth. As I said earlier, when Adam and Eve sinned, it affected the whole earth. I believe that is the reason we have hurricanes, tornadoes, storms, blizzards, etc. We call them natural disasters, but I personally believe they are inspired by the evil one. I believe all four seasons were given to man as a blessing. I do not believe God is the one who causes natural disasters. I believe Satan is the one who causes natural disasters. I believe God permits or allows them to happen, but I do not believe God is the agent behind them.

Throughout human history God has been dealing with man step-by-step. God is a God of order. God requires us to do everything decently and in order.

1 Corinthians 14:40 *Let all things be done decently and in order.*

THE BIBLE AS A KEY TO LIFE

After Adam sinned, God had to find another way to bring man back into a rightful relationship with Him. As a result, the drama of human history has been continuing for sometime. Man is a creature of time. God knows the past, the present, and the future. God knows the future in totality; we do not. We must trust him every step of the way. Most Bible scholars and theologians tell us the Bible was translated from Hebrew and Greek, old testament from Hebrew, and New Testament from Greek. I believe God inspirited man to write the Bible.

> **2 Peter 1:21** *For the prophecy came not in old time by the will of man: but holy men of God spake as they were moved by the Holy Ghost.*

I believe the Bible was given to man so that man would know something about his past, present, and future. The Bible charts man's course now and for eternity. With the Bible, man can know what course he is heading into. It is a guide for man. The Bible was given to man for man to know right from wrong. The Bible states there is a way that seems right unto a man, but that way is the way of death.

> **Proverbs 3:6** *In all thy ways acknowledge Him and He shall direct thy paths.*

> **Psalms 37:5** *Commit thy ways unto the Lord, trust also in Him and He shall bring it to pass.*

> **Jude 1:11** *Woe unto them! For they have gone in the way of Cain, and ran greedily after the error of Balaam for reward, and perished in the gainsaying of Core.*

> **James 5:20** *Let him know, that he which converteth the sinner from the error of his way shall save a soul from death, and shall hide a multitude of sins.*

WHY WAS THE BIBLE GIVEN TO MANKIND?

The Bible is the most treasured possession a man has; it is man's anchor for life. God inspired different men to write the Bible, (his Holy Word). These writings were given for all future generations. With these writings man can know whether he is in line with his creator and fellowman. The Bible was given to man so that he would have a clear-cut view of his eternal destiny. Man will live eternally with God in heaven if he or she is born again. If a person does not know Jesus Christ as his personal Lord and Savior, he will spend eternity in a devil's hell. It is that simple; there is no middle ground. The Bible was given to man so that he could avoid that dreadful place called hell. The Bible states, God said "I do not wish any should perish."

2 Peter 3:9 ... *Not willing that any should perish, but that all should come to repentance.*

CHAPTER TEN

THE THREE MAJOR DECISIONS IN LIFE

As we live up on planet earth, we must make many decisions, some which can be very difficult. Yet, we all must make decisions whether good or bad. I believe there are three key decisions a person will make while he or she lives. They may not necessarily be in the same order, however I do believe the majority of people will make these three decisions at some point in their lives.

<u>Number One</u>: *Choosing their eternal destiny.* God has given all people the capacity to make decisions or choices in this life that will affect their eternal location. I believe where a people will spend eternity is not a light matter. In fact, I believe it is the most important decision one will make throughout the course of their lives. Of course, this comes by way of the new birth should one desire to make heaven their home. If one chooses not to accept Jesus as their Lord and Savior, the alternative is to spend eternity in hell. With this decision there is no middle ground, none, none, none; it is either heaven or hell. The Lord has promised us our life time years upon the earth, after which we surely die, then we enter our eternal destination.

Psalms 90:10 *The days of our years are three score years and ten; and if by reason of strength they be fourscore years, yet is their strength labour and sorrow; for it is soon cut off, and we fly away.*

When we compare our years on earth with eternity, our life's time counts as nothing. Our minds cannot fully comprehend eternity, for it is too far out for us. As the Bible states, "Today, is the day of salvation."

Luke 3:6 *And all flesh shall see the salvation of God.*

And all shall see the salvation of God.

2 Thessalonians 2:13 *But we are bound to give thanks always to God for you, brethren beloved of the Lord, because God hath from the beginning chosen you to salvation through sanctification of the Spirit and belief of the truth:*

From the Scriptures the Bible gives us a beautiful picture of heaven: peace, joy, love, happiness, no more crying, no more worries, a perfect environment.

Deuteronomy 33:13 *And of Joseph he said, Blessed of the Lord be his land, for the precious things of heaven, for the dew, and for the deep that coucheth beneath,*

2 Corinthians 5:14 *For we know that if our earthly house of this tabernacle were dissolved, we have a building of God, an house not made with hands, eternal in the heavens.*

Revelations 21:1 *And I saw a new heaven and a new earth: for the first heaven and the first earth were passed away; and there was no more sea.*

2 *And I John saw the holy city, new Jerusalem, coming down from God out of heaven, prepared as a bride adorned for her husband.*

3 *And I heard a great voice out of heaven saying, Behold the tabernacle of God is with men, and he will dwell with them and they shall be his people, and God himself shall be with them and be their God.*

4 *And God shall wipe away all tears from their eyes; and there shall be no more death, neither sorrow, neither crying, neither shall there be any more pain: for the former things are passed away.*

The Lord allows each person to decide his or her own destiny—hell or heaven. I do hope you choose heaven.

The Bible also tells us about a place called hell. From scripture we can gather that this place exists. God tells us in his word, I do not wish any should perish.

John 3:16 *for God so loved the world, that he gave his only begotten Son, that whosoever believes in him should not perish, but have everlasting life.*

1 Corinthians 1:18 *For the preaching of the cross is to them that perish foolishness; but unto us which are saved it is the power of God.*

2 Peter 3:9 *The Lord is not slack concerning his promise, as some men count slackness; but long-suffering to us-ward, not willing that any should perish, but that all should come to repentance.*

Here are some scriptures on hell:

Luke 16:23 *And he lifted up his eyes, being in torments, and seeth Abraham afar off, and Lazarus in his bosom.*

> **Revelation 1:18** *I am he that liveth, and was dead; and behold I am alive for evermore, Amen; and have the keys of hell and of death.*
>
> **Matthew 10:28** *And fear not them which kill the body, but are not able to kill the soul: rather fear him which is able to destroy both soul and body in hell.*

Remember, the title of this book, the Bible as a key to life. I hope you choose life, I hope you choose heaven. The decision is yours alone. Only you can make this ultimate decision concerning where you spend eternity. That is awesome, and at the same time a sobering reality.

<u>**Number Two:**</u> **Choosing a mate.** I believe when a person makes a decision on a mate, he or she is making a big decision that will affect their entire life. While I write this book, I am a single Christian male. This is one area in which I have sought the Lord very seriously, for I believe it can have either a favorable or adverse affect upon my total life. God made woman and man for each other. Man and woman go together like water is wet. It is just normal and natural for a man to be attracted to a woman, and for a woman to be attracted to a man. God made us that way. We have a built-in desire for each other. However, in order to please God, we must involve God in choosing a life partner. If we do not do it God's way, we are apt to suffer severe consequences. Therefore, it is crucial that we follow God standards as outlined in the Holy Bible...

> **1 Timothy 5:14** *I will therefore that the younger women marry, bear children, guide the house, give none occasion to the adversary to speak reproachfully.* **5:15** *For some are already turned aside after Satan.*
>
> **1 Corinthians 7:2** *Nevertheless, to avoid fornication, let every man have his own wife, and let every woman have her own husband.*

THE THREE MAJOR DECISIONS IN LIFE

1 Thessalonians 4:3 *For this is the will of God, even your sanctification, that ye should abstain from fornication:*

When one makes the decision to be married, it affects his lifestyle either positively or negatively. Choosing a mate is serious business. I firmly suggest a person seek the Lord's guidance if he wishes to marry. Here are some scriptures on choosing a husband and a wife.

Hebrews 13:4 *Marriage is honorable and all, and the bed undefiled: but whoremongers and adulterers God will judge.*

1 Corinthians 7:9 *But if they cannot contain, let them marry: for it is better to marry than to burn.*

Luke 14:20 *And another said, I have married a wife and therefore I cannot come.*

I hope these Scriptures will guide you as you seek the Lord in this area.

<u>Number Three:</u> Choosing or deciding upon a job or a career. How you earn your living is as equally paramount decision to involve God with. Remember, once man fell in the garden of Eden, the work principle was started.

Genesis 3:23 *Therefore the Lord God sent him forth from the garden of Eden to till the ground from whence he was taken.*

Bible also states, if a man does not work neither shall he eat.

1 Thessalonians 4:11 *And that ye study to be quiet, and to do your own business, and to work with your own hands, as we commanded you;*

> **2 Thessalonians 3:10** *For even when we were with you, this we commanded you, that if any would not work, neither should he eat.*

The work principal is scriptural whether we like it or not. We must earn our living by performing some kind of job function in this life. I believe this is also an area, in which we should firmly seek the Lord. I believe people are much happier when they enjoy what they do. Sadly, many people work just for money; they really do not like what they are doing. Money can never totally fulfill us; we need to be involved in something we really enjoy doing. This life is too short for us to settle and merely go through the motions of making a living, when we were designed for a much greater purpose. This is precisely why this is a critical area in which we should seek God's help and direction with.

CHAPTER ELEVEN

JESUS, THE MAN WHO MASTERED LIFE

I like to refer to Jesus, as the man who mastered life. When we talk about life, in this sense, it is a very broad subject. Life is composed of many different elements. Jesus is the center and core of life for the human race. Without Jesus's coming to the earth, to redeem mankind, man would be eternally lost. I think about what God the father has done for us through Jesus. It is too mysterious and too wonderful for the human mind to conceive. Just think for a moment, Jesus is a part of the Godhead; he always was, and always will be. God the father, with his great love for mankind, took Jesus out of heaven to come to earth in order to redeem all men. Our all wise and sovereign God impregnated a Virgin named Mary, by the Holy Spirit, to bring mankind a Savior to the world. We cannot fully understand, explain, or know all the details about the virgin birth, but we do know it was a miracle based on God's holy Word.

> **Luke 1:26** *And in the sixth month the angel Gabriel was sent from God unto a city of Galilee, named Nazareth,* **27** *To a virgin espoused to a man whose name was Joseph, of the house of David; and the virgin's name was Mary.* **28** *And the angel came in unto her, and said, Hail, thou*

art highly favoured, the Lord is with thee: blessed art thou amongst women.

29 *And when she saw him, she was troubled at his saying, and cast in her mind what manner of salutation this should be.*

30 *And the angel said unto her, Fear not, Mary: for thou hast found favour with God.*

31 *And, behold, thou shalt conceive in thy womb, and bring forth a son, and shalt call his name JESUS.*

32 *He shall be great, and shall be called the Son of the Highest: and the Lord God shall give unto him the throne of his father David:*

33 *And he shall reign over the house of Jacob for ever; and of his kingdom there shall be no end.*

34 *Then said Mary unto the angel, How shall this be, seeing I know not a man?*

35 *And the angel answered and said unto her, The Holy Ghost shall come upon thee, and the power of the Highest shall overshadow thee: therefore also that holy thing which shall be born of thee shall be called the Son of God.*

36 *And, behold, thy cousin Elisabeth, she hath also conceived a son in her old age: and this is the sixth month with her, who was called barren.*

37 *For with God nothing shall be impossible.*

38 *And Mary said, Behold the handmaid of the Lord; be it unto me according to thy word. And the angel departed from her.*

Jesus was both God and man while he walked the earth. That, too, is difficult to understand or explain, but I believe it with my whole heart. I believe that Jesus ministered to people while he walked the earth, I believe he ministered as a Prophet anointed by the Spirit of God. Jesus did not minister to people as the son of God. That could be mind boggling to the natural human fleshly mind, but I believe it to be true.

Luke 2:52 *And Jesus increased in wisdom and stature, and in favor with God and man.*

Ephesians 4:13 *Till we all come in the unity of the faith, and of the knowledge of the son of God, unto a perfect man, unto the measure of the stature of the fullness of Christ:*

If Jesus were tempted in all points as we are, yet without sin, he had the capacity to yield to sin or temptation, but he did not yield to any kind of sin. Jesus experienced the same kinds of temptations we experience daily, but the key is Jesus did not yield to them, not a one. In order to be the world's savior he had to experience temptation in order to redeem mankind. He experienced temptation as a man anointed by the Spirit of God.

Matthew 4:1 *Then was Jesus led up of the Spirit into the wilderness to be tempted of the devil.*
2 And when he had fasted forty days and forty nights, he was afterward an hungred.
3 And when the tempter came to him, he said, If thou be the Son of God, command that these stones be made bread.
4 But he answered and said, It is written, Man shall not live by bread alone, but by every word that proceedeth out of the mouth of God.
5 Then the devil taketh him up into the holy city, and setteth him on a pinnacle of the temple,
6 And saith unto him, If thou be the Son of God, cast thyself down: for it is written, He shall give his angels charge concerning thee: and in their hands they shall bear thee up, lest at any time thou dash thy foot against a stone.
7 Jesus said unto him, It is written again, Thou shalt not tempt the Lord thy God.

8 *Again, the devil taketh him up into an exceeding high mountain, and sheweth him all the kingdoms of the world, and the glory of them;*
9 *And saith unto him, All these things will I give thee, if thou wilt fall down and worship me.*
10 *Then saith Jesus unto him, Get thee hence, Satan: for it is written, Thou shalt worship the Lord thy God, and him only shalt thou serve.*
11 *Then the devil leaveth him, and, behold, angels came and ministered unto him.*

Jesus mastered life as a man anointed by the Spirit of God. Jesus mastered life totally and completely in every area without any exception. Jesus mastered life as my personal Lord and Savior and your personal Lord and Savior! We are following a leader, a champion, our soon-to-be coming king. The reason Jesus can be the world's Savior, is that he mastered life for mankind in the earth realm. No other man on earth mastered life the way Jesus did. Jesus is the key to life. Without Jesus, mankind would not have any hope at all.

ABOUT THE AUTHOR

Ernest "Tut" Groover was born in Millen, Georgia. He attended Aaron Elementary School and Burgess Landrum High School. Upon graduation from high school, he moved to Fort Lauderdale, Florida where he began working as a shipping and receiving clerk at Colonial Plastic Company in Pompano Beach, Florida for about nine months.

In June, 1969, he began working at Bell South Corporation (now known as AT&T). In December, 1976, he was promoted to management. He then attended Broward Community College in Fort Lauderdale, Florida. in June, 1994, he retired from Bell South corporation, with 25 years of service. He ran a multi-million dollar coin telephone collection's operations for Bell South for almost 20 years in South Florida. After leaving Bell South corporation he spent 3.5 years in retirement.

In November, 1997 he started working for the Broward County School District (located in Fort Lauderdale, Florida), as a teachers assistant. He retired from the Broward County Schools District in August, of 2012.

Currently, he is an ordained Ruling Elder at Ascension Peace Presbyterian Church in Lauderhill, Florida, where he teaches the adult class. He is both a member of the Christian education committee and a member of the finance committee. He served as chairman of the board of trustees for 12 years. He also served as a deacon for three years. He participated in the choir for 25 years and was President of the men's organization for seven years.

He is presently working on his future writings and inventions.

www.ingramcontent.com/pod-product-compliance
Lightning Source LLC
Chambersburg PA
CBHW052122110526
44592CB00013B/1707